street pieces

poems & prose poems

gregory k. robinson

WESTRON PRESS
P.O. BOX 5285
TOLEDO, OHIO 43611-0285

This is a signed and numbered edition.
This is copy number:

218

cover design by
zita sodieka

acknowledgments:
i would like to gratefully thank and
acknowledge john roth, for all his support and help
in editing these gravelly street pieces and bearing
with me on those long drives through the concrete
forests and the greasy food diners where waitresses
go to die and sad faces go to sip the romanticized
past through greasy coffee cups and day old cream. i
would like to thank my wife lisa, for attending those
"early years" poetry reads, my family and friends for
all their help and support in all my academic
adventures o' fun! special thanks to zita sodieka for
the cover and westron press for their vision of the
"real" poetry of real america. finally, i would like to
acknowledge my dead mentors: jack kerouac and
walt whitman...they rocked! and most importantly
thank you God!
        -this book is dedicated to the street saints
with dirty faces!

"no good deed goes unpunished"

WESTRON PRESS

contents

street pieces 1

once upon a time... 7

the fairy godmother 11

the nursery rhyme that shouldn't have 14

the peasant whose message remained in the glass bottle 15

title: "little red's labyrinth or..." 17

oz revisited 18

miracles 20

life amazed 21

snow what? 22

grand...ma again? 23

butterflies with touched wings don't fly no more 24

street spiels 26

the three little pigs and the big bad-assed wolf that blew 28

moxey: the street rag doll 30

yes, santa claus, there is a virginia 32

sweeping beauty 34

me myself and i 37

trick or treat? 40

a non-story 41

just another story retold 43

the edge 46

let's get lost 49

death by time 54

street dreams 56

kites 67

street pieces

i am the teller of the tale,
the narrator with superficial commentary,
the behind the scenes reporter of the 11 o'clock news,
the motivator of changing insight,
the fool, the lost dream collector,
from fall to experience,
the undertaker of the journey
into the brutalities of the street,
sick and tired of life.
but the madness of it all drives me on,
to understand this home, this city,
is to understand life,
after all this is america,
and everybody's doing what they're supposed to do,
or so they think,
the dirty muse is on me now again,
and it's name is any name in the city.

this is dedicated to the street saints with dirty faces,
who work their magic goodness,
each day in the mean city,
and with each breath,
and who don't always let the system get to them,
and who somehow manage to warm the cold dead back
                                        alleys,
and who make a corner safe for a while,
and who just try to stand up to the street,
and who try to try, and sometimes cry,
and try to offer a way out,

1

and who acknowledge the horror of it all,
and who have great courage and honesty,
and believe such words,
and who don't fall from their purpose,
and who don't allow no one else to fall
through the cracks of broken dreams in the street pieces,
for goodness sake!

outside my duplex rolls the infamous swan creek,
only a few feet deep,
and deadly polluted,
there ain't no mermaids in the water
that leads to the maumee river,
which leads to lake erie,
on to the st. lawrence seaway,
then to the atlantic ocean,

people say if you spit in it,
it'll travel to everywhere there's water,
that creek ain't no mississippi river,
but it is escape,
as it gurgles and calls you from the darkness
deep from sleepless city-night street lights,
to ride its holy waves outta here.

the dead end streets, my dead end street,
runs north and south and butts up to that creek,
the railroad tracks go east and west,
that run along side that creek,
over which thunder trains can be heard,
creaking and rumblin' through the night
on rusted rails that seemingly go on and on,
forever and ever,

2

straight forward
into new horizons,
and you can see the train's headlamp,
wincing and winking at you,
through the trees, the menacing vines at night,
with whistles calling you to join them,
if you dare.

only a few blocks from these dead end streets
is the freeway, that drives driven people places, fast,
although not during, (that uncanny phrase), rush hour.
the highway used to be smooth and free,
littered with materialistic billboards of naive consumerism,
once, like all the highways of america in the fifties,
upon a romanticized time ago,
america itself was made from poured slabs of sweat,
and minerals,
and american freedom was ridden to faster speeds,
go man go, a green light of expression and ideas,
to go on forward, on and on,
what are you waiting for? as if it asked you,
nihilism with a happily ever after ending?

but there i sat,
spinning my wheels,
to the pulse of the road, of the street,
of life itself in characteristic america,
and the prose-poetry of a whole new road opened up to me,
and its' pulse jabbed through my veins
forever infecting my whole system,
the very street built by americans,
that leads to other streets and other americas,
and other americans who were trapped by their own curbs,

and handicapped zones,
and who would never feel the rhythm
of life, of the open road,
until now!
and now, the proverbial piper
has called you to join him
on the open roads, the streets.

but there aren't really any escapes,
if we choose to leave,
the planes up in the friendly skies,
fly above the streets,
to here and to there, nearly everywhere,
way up there, aesthetically safe, and pure,
with the angels.
but they're not really friendly skies at all,
'cause they bring you back,
back down to the towns and the cities and the streets,
in which there are no more escapes,
no more causeways, freeways, byways,
or throughways that go to, and through to, the sky.
even the trains don't really carry passengers anymore,
just freight, with trucks piggybacked on top,
and all the roads that lead away from the city,
lead to some other city,
the same city really, but with different spellings,
a fucking mega-megatropolis across this land,
which was made for you and me.

sitting, listening to my wheezing breath,
i sucked in this invisible thing we call air,
but it is visible in the city,
and it's here like me,

like me and the stagnant air, stuck here,
as the sun exits for a night or forever,
depending on how scared you are of the darkness,
and the horror as you watch the bloodsucking streets
come alive from the dead:
hookers, little girls, old ladies in faded print dresses,
late night men, teenagers runnin', children who survive,
all there, the living dead,
past the broken, paved promises and street rubble,
beyond all signs, traffic noises, and gas smells,
and the rusted car parts,
that have fallen on these open graves called streets,
marked with patched tar tombstones,
in this place we call home.

pristine cars once rode the roads,
now barely start without a prayer,
people drive, ride, then die,
such is our purpose in the city,
everyone loved the streets, seen through car windows,
but for now the traffic jams suck life from our time,
emit vomit fumes, and time wears at everything,
except the steel sewer covers,
manhole covers, womanhole covers,
whatever, as they lay there,
laughing hard at my nothing problems,
i have no choice,
the streets call me and i survive,

the broken concrete, red bricks, asphalt, and pavement
broken messages,
broken american dreams,
the traffic is already at play in the streets,

but the sun ain't up, the long night continues,
yet, the tall breathtaking cloudmakers,
billow smoke from the factories,
hide the sun from us for a while longer,
the whole city feeds, lives off of the streets,
from here to manhattan to chicago to l.a., the bronx, toledo,
to detroit, birthplace of our poisonous heritage,
hotly, we ride out polluted passions,
our cars,

in search of freedom,
freedom of self-expression,
the leashing and unleashing of brave thoughts,
through talks, and loves, and kicks,
in pursuit of some self-centered
manumit of societal norms,
life is life, and kind is kind,
but to take one more magnificent trip
away from the city, and from it all...
but no! the city doesn't end,
we know that because we go on from one street to another,
the pieces connect,
the once proud poured and flattened and smoothed over
                                        roads
are now reduced to street pieces.

once upon a time...

...there once was a mean city.
and a boy who lived alone in the mean city.

he had no friends but he had courage and he is the hero of this
story.

on a dreary autumn morning he woke shivering from the chill
of the night. the window had been broken or shot, he couldn't
remember and he didn't really care. the city sounds were loud
and scary but he was used to it.

the boy dressed himself and made a cold breakfast of whatever
he could find between the cans of beer and a bag of chips, then
told his mom goodbye and that he loved her. she yelled at him,
told him to be quiet because she was sick, and didn't want him
to wake up the man who spent the night and had hit her and
yelled at her. the boy left for school. he never wanted to drink
like her and that man did. the place always smelled sour and
old, he thought.

a wino who lived in the streets caught the boy by his worn
collar and demanded money. the boy said "no" and the man
slapped him on the ears and the boy said "okay" and reached
in his pocket and the man let go of his collar and the boy ran
away until his stomach hurt.

the boy met other boys, older than him, who weren't gonna go
to no school. they were working for a man who paid them for
sellin' stuff. the boy had seen what happened to people who
bought the stuff. the boys teased the boy and he fought back

and ran away and they followed after him and the boy nearly cried. "school ain't gonna help you, you is wrong and you is dead if you ever come by our turf again," they screamed.

the boy ducked into a store and shook. the boys waited outside for a while, then went back to their corner to sell stuff to the rich people who had no hope and the poor addicts seeking thrills.

the boy was about to leave the store when the manager pushed him around and yelled at him "for bringing trouble around his place," and told him to "keep outta here!"

the boy left the shop and met two ladies who teased him and wanted him to go with them into a hotel and "make him a man." the boy was excited but scared because he knew that that wasn't no love. no love like the love he had seen on t.v. or the kind of love his grandmother had told him about in fairy tales. the street ladies grabbed him and he said "okay" and then pointed down the street and said, "it's them, they there, it's the cops." the girls gathered themselves and hurried down the street, lost in the early morning shadows of some back alley.

the boy walked on until the rain poured down and soaked his torn old jacket that didn't fit no more anyhow.

he shivered.

the boy hurried to make the bell but he was late and he had to go down to the office and he sat and heard all about "bein' responsible and acting like a young man and on and on they scolded him for this and told him he'd never amount to nothin'

8

if he didn't start working and getting to school on time" and on and on he heard this until he could've cried.

then they let him go to class and the teacher gave him a nasty look and the kids teased him for being soaked and being late and being dressed in torn, old clothes. the boy ignored them and got to work on some reading and didn't do so well but he tried anyhow.

the boy's stomach growled and he couldn't wait for lunch.

and then an announcement came over the speaker for "all the students to go to the auditorium for an assembly."

the boy's stomach growled louder than before.

the assembly was about "saying no to drugs and alcohol," and the woman who spoke was dressed real pretty and she kept tellin' the kids to just "say no" and that was all she'd say, "just say no," and not run or lie or trick your way outta trouble and the boy was troubled by this and he ate lunch fast, very fast, because it was monday and he really hadn't eaten since last friday's lunch in the cafeteria.

the boy went to class and did the very best he could.

the boy went home a different way and didn't see the boys, the worn girls left him alone being too busy with a nice car parked along the curb, they didn't pay him no mind. later, at home, his mom was fighting and arguing with some other man, and the man hit the boy for trying to stop the fight.

the boy went to his room and put some cardboard over the

window and it barely covered the hole and then read some
books as best he could until he fell asleep.

the boy lived and survived in the mean city, the ugly city, and
had no real friends but he did have courage and was the hero
of this story.

the fairy godmother

once upon a time, or late last spring in this mean city, a fairy godmother got hired by the county to change the world, or so she thought, yet she was young, and not very street smart, but she really wanted to help, save the children, make families whole again, within the confines of the system of course,

her goal was to get everything needy people wanted and every want they needed, in the name of the idealistic goodness, and even possibly get more than she ever dreamed of, or reasonably hoped for, and she had a brave heart, lovely and quaint and frail, in her hand she held a list of people who needed her, and in her other hand she had a magic wand, and lamp to grant wishes, and special bells, and a spring in her step, and a crimson carriage to drive through the streets, she also had a college degree, not a terrible waste at all, but oops, they forgot to teach her about people, and politics and problems, and the streets with their sharp pieces, but no matter, she was a quick learner, cum laude, in case you didn't know,

her first stop and no bodies home, not a soul. the family left, tipped off that she was comin',

her second stop, almost stopped her cold dead in a standoff, with a lord who drank too much but who eventually put his gun away, and called off his pit-bull dragons, she left fast, shaken, she cried to her supervisor at the office, and he called the police for her, (she couldn't dial the phone), they removed the children, and arrested the big, mean man, who threatened to kill her, after he sobered up (he was out after he sobered up, on his own recognizance), later that afternoon, nobody told her about that, and the fact that the lord of this castle promised to be nice to everyone, and never drink again, and...well he said he'd do it, and the kids were back home later, and the family was reunited, pending court date, a hundred years from now,

the fairy godmother seemed lost, she tried her magic wand, maybe the batteries were low? already? she ate a nauseous lunch, with other fairy godmothers, who told her their bedtime stories about the trenches, and those stories were worse than hers, and that made her feel afraid, they also reminded her to buy a suede leather coat, to keep the cockroaches from laying golden eggs in her clothes,

later, her last case involved an old lady, a mother, (for lack of a better word), actually, a stepmother of four of the six children, who all lived in this shoe, in this mean city, once upon a near quittin' time, but the fairy godmother was dedicated, and visited the stepmother of these kids,

she met the youngest of the six, who asked for three wishes: love, slippers, and a prince, but the fairy godmother couldn't come through, and the girl cried and said, "she lied," the fairy social worker couldn't make them wishes come true, her wand was definitely broken, and would probably need to go to the shop, and the lamp was burned-out, already? cheap bulbs, and the bells stopped tinkling in the spring breeze,

besides, the stepmother had the custody papers, in her fat twisted hands, and the fairy godmother social worker bitch couldn't touch those kids, or remove them from that home,

and none of the wishes were granted that day, and the fairy

godmother went home, ready to quit, and well that's the end of the story...or so you thought,

for the fairy godmother still works downtown, and she still tried her wand now and again, (even though it still really doesn't work at all), and she traded in her carriage for a v.w. bug that still runs well, slightly rusted, and she does what she can, in her brown suede leather trench coat, and instead of three wishes, she grants three needs: food, a bed, some clothes, (clean or not), that's all the magic she can do, but she does try and try and...as she lives, survives, sort of happily, ever after.

the nursery rhyme that shouldn't have

there was this little miss muffet like cute girl with pigtails and a bright print dress who sat down on a tuffet, (or something comfortable), eating her curds and whey, (probably some cold cereal or maybe even something sweet), when along came this sick little spider dude who sat down beside her and asked her to go with him back to his house, to his basement to play.

well, she knew him because he was nice to all the kids in the neighborhood and all the parents even liked him too, so she wasn't frightened away because he wouldn't hurt her and she knew him and he wasn't no stranger, but what he did to her was strange–that ass hole—and unhappily ever after she was never the same!

the peasant whose message remained in the glass bottle

the old man hobbled with his cane and torn overcoat along the uneven and faded red brick street down to the old school yard and he asked himself the reasons why? it was cold and icy out on the lonely dark road as the night rain finally ceased yet left a hazy mist which blurred his vision.

he cried alone.

"why did everyone move out of here? this used to be a good neighborhood. why didn't they stay and live like i did? why did they cover parts of the street with tar instead of fixin' up the old bricks with new ones? why did everything change and everyone i knew leave here? why did they close my old high school? why did my wife leave me? why did my family leave me? what did i do? i want to know why?"

the old man stepped off the broken pavement and bricks in the mud and the grassy knolls of the high school's back yard. he looked around and felt safe. sirens blared and he remained immune, aloof.

"why did they interfere with me? why did they all try and get me to stop? why did my wife and family leave me? i want to know why?"

he sat down on the cold blocks of cement. he curled up on the back entrance stoop of the old school.

"it was right here, when i was sixteen years old and sittin' here after school with my old friends, and me, when i first took to having fun and drinking and all. why did everyone get on me about that? why did my family leave? why did everyone leave? i want to know why?"

the back alley street lights were all broken and the old man couldn't see past the gnarled trees or the bushes or past his very own past. his eyes didn't even look at what his hands were doing; years and years of habit. he licked his lips and pulled out a half pint of wine and drank it down and died right there on that old back entrance way stoop, by that old condemned high school in that old neighborhood. that's where it all happened, right back there. that's where it all ended and began right back there way back when, and for why?

i want to know why?

title: "little red's labyrinth or the long walk; which, like life itself is difficult and often scary, that is, if you're driving down some long and winding road and suddenly you'd have to walk because your carriage or car breaks down on the freeway, and then you'd have to cut through the dying heart of the city through the worst part of the concrete forest late at night on your way to grandma's house, who still lives in a padlocked home in the real 'hood; and your eyes and ears play tricks on you and you can't tell whether or not the shadows are wolves or woodsmen or was that noise a howl or the wind? maybe you'd better hurry..."

shh!
what's that?
shh! keep walking,
too late,
bang!
dead...

oz revisited

somewhere under the rainbow,
skies aren't blue,
there's a land that i heard of,
once in a horrible lullaby,

they discharged her
from the emerald wing of the wizard's hospital,
the former mental patient,
from her ward sweet ward,
where all the colors worked,
once upon a time,
when she found her lost toto,

now forced to live in the lost streets
of the not-so-emerald-city,
far from kansas,
clicking her ruby-red keds,
and singing to herself,
as lollipop kids beat her, then rob her,

down the darkened yellow stained road,
washed from the dull street-lights,
as people in their composite plastic horses
of a different color,
whine, honk their horns, and drive away,
barely missing her,

the good fairy queens, the hookers,
ignore her,
being too far gone, even for them,
everyone passes her with rusted hearts,

straw brains, and lost courage,
no one helped,
even the wicked witch didn't fuck with her,

as nightmarish flying sandstone monkey gargoyles,
from high atop the old abandoned buildings,
tortured her mind,
her anti-technicolor thoughts,

but hopefully,
someone will give her a x-mas dinner,
and not send her out into the wet chilling night,

let's elect someone to make our problem go away,
arrest her, arrest her,
keep her out of sight and mind,
is the wizard home?
he can help,

but the sewers back up,
with the wet frustration
of what she once was,
as she clicked her heels together hard,
three times and cried,
"there's no place like being alone,
there's no place like being alone."
now lost forever,
somewhere between kansas and hell.

miracles

sometimes i like the city,
even at night,

when distant sirens wail,
and nearby traffic throbs,
and the rhythm of the streets echo
from back speakers of a rusted pontiac,

yet there, right there,
in that littered park,
can you see the people standing, drinking,
that is,
if you live long enough for your eyes to adjust

see 'em, look hard,
see the sparkling eyes of people,
playin' ball,
all day, shootin' hoops,
and not each other,
all standing together
in front of dim headlights,

today was a good day
-for the city

life amazed

on his way home from a business trip he took a detour into the heart of the city and late into the night in which he drove around in his chic red sports car for hours past the characters who hung out near the adult bookstores and the winos who looked past him with their glazed empty eyes and the dead end street people who wandered through the darkness and who didn't live anywhere near where he lived and the dressed strippers who waited outside the club for the owner to open it up so they could get undressed in front of the men who paid them to play out their symbolized fantasies and yet he drove past them all and drove and drove until finally he mustered the courage to live his choice, to ride the streets of the midnight dreams of his quest; and yet, the signs prophesied his decision, he ignored the signs: a church steeple with its bent cross rusted and now barely visible in the cloud-veiled moonlight and a torn bible tossed on a plastic garbage can, or the smile from a female grill cook who saw him through the windows as she served yet another on duty police officer in a late night diner and the man drove and drove until he was driven to drive past a rescue mission house in which he almost stopped because he heard singing...

"i once was lost/but now am found..."

...but then, he finally found what he was looking for, his grace, she had appeared in that hour and he believed that and all was well and he attended to his quest and in the heat of the moment of his bought and paid intimacy he fed his nocturnal desires, a precious princess sold herself to him for his burning desires; then he dropped her off at the empty lonely corner where the broken street-lights faded into pain.

snow what?

mirror, mirror,
on the roach-infested project's bathroom wall,
who's the saddest one of them all?
"we are," said the mirror...

or did it?

grand...ma again?

you know that broken old woman who lived alone in the woods, just north of the storybook 'hood, where that old woman sits at home, alone, and watches t.v., and is happy once in a while and who had 'ready raised her kids, suddenly had another mouth to feed and a diaper to change and a mess to clean up, while that young bio-mother dropped off her child and went out the back way to the bars away from it all, to get herself some freedom from all the noise and diapers and mess and work and stuff that comes with babies...

damn!

butterflies with touched wings don't fly no more

little butterfly, little girl,
someone's little child,
once upon a lifetime ago,
held once,
in a woven cocoon on a solitary bough,
once upon a-not-so-many days ago,

it was at summer's end,
when the cold street winds blew then,
when, either abused or addicted or both,
she fluttered once, and for a moment flew,
then,
fell onto the pavement of a wet november night,

and now men, pimps, insects crawl out to her,
teach her to fly again,
only this time for them,
from street corner to street corner,
from manless boy to manless man,
from moonless night to empty daylight,
from sickened pleasures to dark delights,

whatever they pay her to do,
dust,

and buses go by,
fifty cents to ride,
the price of her salvation?
but she stays instead,
forever now on any darkened street corner,

24

with inviting eyes, light less, hurt,
smiles at us,
"wanta date?"
"no thanks,"
and part of me watches her die,
and her eyes meet mine,
then turns away,

worn,
she sells her loss
to the sad night,
paying dearly for her childhood's cost,
flightless and without hope,
seduced,
forever in her ruined cocoon,
attached to some corner of some nameless street,
the lights shine of the city,
someone touched her,
strong hands turned her dreams,
her wings,
to dust,

(and time shed a tear for another child.)

street spiels

there's a street,
and nothing down there done lives there,
and nobody ever goes there,
man, a place so bad
even the cops won't fuck with anyone from around there,

some say ghosts hang there,
down that dark old alley,
ghosts of dead pimps,
and sour drug dealers,
and smelly hookers
and mean-assed winos,
and people who liked fighting and killing,
and people whose spirits are so bad
that even hell doesn't ever want them hanging around any
                                                        more!

that place is fucked,
things, uncool things,
keep happening down there,
cars starting up that didn't work no more,
and this street music comes on from somewhere;
haunting and mean,
and girls dancin',
and men drinking and gambling,
and everyone swearing,
voices,
echoing voices talking,
and laughing and what-not-such-nonsense be happening,
that all the neighbors moved away,
and all the factories closed up around that alley,

26

and all the streets moved too,
and nobody alive goes there,
near those streets,
the dark alleys of the concrete forest of
the mean city,
that is until the sun comes up
and the spirits go away,

and as with death, mourning comes,
you can tell 'cause the street-lights go off,
and the city arises from its' active slumber.

the three little pigs and the big bad-assed wolf that blew

once upon a time, or last week i think,
there lived a big bad-assed wolf dude,
he wasn't real, the politicians all said,
but he was real, and he bit too!

anyhow, he went to look about his neighborhood,
and soon came to a house,
the house of the first pig,
and it was made out of straw,

and nothin' kept it up really,
no foundation, no family, no laughter, no love,
and the wolf just huffed and the house fell,
and the first pig died, so the wolf ate him up,

then the wolf went to look about some more in his
neighborhood,
and he soon came to another house,
the house of the second pig,
and it was made out of sticks,

weak sticks, unkept, filthy, and unpainted,
depressed and lonely, the pig that lived there,
lived in fear of the neighborhood,
and the wolf huffed and puffed and the house fell,
and the second pig died, so the wolf ate him up,

then the wolf went to look around some more in his
neighborhood,
and he soon came to another house,
the house of the third pig,

this house everyone left alone,
because this house was a magic house,
and if it fell,
it would move down the street the very next day,
and the third pig would be in business as usual,

but the wolf couldn't resist,
so he huffed and puffed and snuffed and sneezed
and blew and blew, again and again until his eyes
watered,
yet the house stayed up,
because it was made out of crack,
and those houses never really fall down for long.

moxey: the street rag doll

there's this old abandoned house,
that some little girl named 'Ella,
who we all used to love and watch walk,
had lived in,
once before upon some time ago,
but she's gone now, moved away from the city,
you know, if i remember right,
not so long upon a time ago,
last year i think, or maybe, who knows?
man, she had the sauciest walk around,
mind you though, we never meant that to be bad,
i bet she didn't even know it,
being so shy and perfect and small,
and innocent,
as innocent as the city gets,

anyways,
she was this spirited little button-eyed doll,
who had it all:
brains, imagination, common sense, bad luck,
too bad she was pretty,
what a pumpkin pie pretty ragamuffin doll,
standin' there at about five foot six,
and weighin' in at about a buck ten,
smilin' and avoidin' playin' doll house
with all them toy boys lookin' for a good time,

one day though,
walking home from school,
some man from the mean streets pulled her string,
twisted her hair,

messed her up real bad,
left her at the bottom of the toy box,
because she was always tellin' him "no,"

but he had his way,
and there she lay,
all teary eyed, in tattered clothes,
with a wispy shred of tufted hair,
all fallen, down on her face,
in the dark shadows, alone,
and nearly dead,

that girl sure learned the hard way,
too bad she was pretty,
like i said, real pretty,
and if i remembers rightly,
sometimes later that week,
all them toy boys wanted to play her after that,
and everyone wanted to make her their gypsy queen,
and her without no queendom,
or much of a life after that,
(as if city stories ever really change).

yes, santa claus, there is a virginia!

on a rainy x-mas eve, a shabbily dressed santa came to play his tarnished bell for charity near an old supermarket in the 'hood. he had been doing this for several years. ding pause ding, went the bell as he tried to get people to plop money in his dull red bucket to help the poor. a few nickels here and maybe a quarter there. santa didn't have to worry about getting robbed that day...there was only a few dollars collected and it was near closing time.

"i don't think i'll take this job again," he mumbled. "there ain't much money to be made. i'm embarrassed to give them my bucket unless i slip in a few more dollars myself.

"besides, i'm sick and tired of kids in their cars flipping me off, or pulling at my beard. damn! i hate being santa. them other santa's got it made. they get to work at the better shopping malls and really rake in the bucks to help the needy. all I got here are needy."

ding pause ding. "merry x-mas," he bellowed to two ladies who looked at him hard.

"did you see his beard?" one commented.

"yes! mangy. i bet he drinks the money," the other whispered.

santa sat down on the cold cement sill of the windows. the wind blew hard and he tried to keep warm by pulling in the red jacket by the collars. it was a costume and not designed for the cold express of the northern jet stream that dipped south from canada. ding pause ding. he sneezed.

"God bless you santa claus. sounds like you have a cold," a small girl said.

"thank you, dear," he replied.

"can I ask you something i want for x-mas?"

"well," santa said as he stood up tall and proud. his

32

belt fell past his waist but he tried to ignore it. "have you been good?" this was the part of the job that the man dressed as santa liked best...playing the magical part of santa claus to a child who really believed in him...santa, that is.

"yes, santa claus, i've been trying to be real good."

"let me guess," santa replied.

the girl smiled patiently.

"i bet you want one of them talking baby dolls. or maybe one of them video games, or one of them tea sets, or maybe some new clothes, or..."

"no," the girl sadly replied, "thank you."

ding pause ding. santa rang his bell merrily then looked into her eyes.

"well then, what do you want for x-mas?" he asked curiously.

"i know you're busy but, i want my mommy to stop drinking and hitting me and my baby brother all the time," she whispered dryly.

santa looked at her and noticed the giant black and blue marks on her face. she did not have on a coat that fit her properly. her eyes were as serious as the stars of the north pole. he sat down on the cold cement window sill and looked past her. the grey skies darkened.

"bye, santa, thank you," she hugged him, shrugged her shoulders, turned and walked across the parking lot down to some dark alley and disappeared into the shadows of the dusk. "i'll leave some milk and cookies for you. bring rudolph, too. we wish you a merry x-mas..." she sang until the howling winds blew fiercely and faded her voice into the echoes of the lost streets.

ding long pause ding. clunk.

santa sat on the cold cement baseboard of the store's window, dropped his bell, and wept.

33

sweeping beauty

there's this very old woman,
who lives in the duplex she owns,
by a busy street, in the mean city,
and she always is seen keeping the sidewalks neat,
as she sweeps them,
daily,
in front of her place, even in the rain,

days,
for days on end,
i 'll drive by her house,
and i see her sweeping away,
the dirt and the dust and the years,

sad story about her, so it seems,
told to me by some of the neighborhood gossips,
who swear it's true.
seems the old woman never leaves her place,
unless it's to go to the store,
and she has lived there for years,
took care of her sickly mother,

and that old lady never left,

except once upon a long time ago,
late one summer, near fall,
she went to the country on this one sunday,
in 1939,
to visit her cousin,
take her some homemade breads,
and share a laugh or two.

and it was about a half a days bus drive,
from the duplex,
and not very far,

that woman met a boy there,
and she loved him,
her handsome prince on a white charger,
well actually he was not so handsome,
son of a farmer,
seasoned of face and hands,
and who didn't really ride a white charger,
but actually drove an old tractor,
but, from that day on,
they made plans,
and she was going to return that very next week,
but her mom told her not to go,
to stay,
and take care of her,
because she was sick and old and alone,

so the woman stayed home
that next sunday,
but walked out to the bus,
to see if the courage would let her leave,
but she thought about her mother,
and instead stayed
and took care of her,
because she was sick and old and lonely,

the daughter watched the bus come,
and go,
without her,
as she swept her steps,

and watched the sun set,
and went to bed,
and never left the duplex again,
except to buy groceries,

now, each past sunday she gets up,
and dressed,
in her sunday best,
and goes outside for the bus,
because she wanted so bad to see her love,
yet, her mother became more sick and more old and more
alone and lonely,
instead, the woman stayed,

stayed home instead,
and swept the old crumbling steps,
again, time passed,
and mother eventually died,
nearly thirty years
after the daughter had met her love,

for years and minutes,
she still dreamed about him,
as she swept the front steps,
alone,
and watched the sun set,
each sunday,
dressed in her very best,
and now stands outside, waiting for the bus,
to take her to see her love,
but she stays,

then she sweeps.

me myself and i

(dedicated to what happened to these three witches, i once
knew, and who shared a needle and an eyeball between them
and who lived down the street in the neighborhood in an old
haunted house that needed a whole lotta paint but they didn't
care about it any ways).

me myself and i,
got so, so very high,
so high in fact,
we thought we could never, ever die,
me myself and i,

me myself and i,
flew to a concert,
a total blitz,
we left the concert,
thought we were straight,
stepped on the gas,
can you guess our fate?
me myself and i,

me myself and i,
went to the park,
bought a hashish pie,
put it in a bowl and smoked it whole,
toked on it 'til we choked on it,
suddenly,
but not to fast,
we felt our brains fry,
as we got high,
from that hashish pie,

me myself and i,

i myself and me,
tripped on some lsd
it took an hour before it hit me,
the red green blue, man
was all I could see,
i myself and me,

me myself and i,
o.d.'d on some codeine, cocaine,
or was it speed,
what does it matter,
who really cares,
i know what i took that morning,
i know it was bad,
but mixed with music and wine,
it made me feel so fine,
the doctor came in and spoke to us,
said he,
we must become straight,
we must never get high,
or surely our brains will surely die,
me myself and i,

me myself and i,
swore i 'd never get high,
so the coke and the joints passed me by,
until one day,
one j.,
did not pass by,
i got high,
me myself and i,

me myself and i,
got up a little to high,
we never came down,
dead end,
fast lane bound,
vegetating away,
me myself and i.

(and they didn't live very happily or very long ever after).

trick or treat?

on the fiery eve of this st. hallow's day,
in the year of our Lord: nineteen hundred and ninety
something,

this year,
even the demons were shocked,
as two inner-city clubs
went on tryin' real hard,
in the name of turf-estate,

all adorned in bright battle array,
cool high tops, sports sweats, and bandanas,
each heavily armed with light weight modern weaponries:
aluminum bats, guns, dirty smiles and cool looks,
to terrorize the 'hood,
where boys learned to kill,
as quick as to die,
as the never ending street story dead-ends,

so the boys were challenged in another drive by shooting,
the shit goes down again in the turfdom,
the battle drums throb,
from someone's boom box,
the slaughter ends as fast as it began,
hot blood is cold and cursed and wet,
melts with rain,
stains the sidewalks
as the night ends,
and the dead lay dead.

a non-story

it was a cold, damp, dark and stormy night near the outer warehouse district of the old south end of a city in the concrete forest. actually, it was not even dark on that particular night. the dry sun was at its zenith. it was a warm afternoon and there were no clouds to be found to contrast against the blue hue of the sky. so it really was not a cold, dark and stormy night after all, but a warm, dry, bright and sunny day.

there was not an old, abandoned, brick warehouse nearby either. its worn red and burnt stones were not smooth from age and weather. the broken windows were not boarded with plywood sheets and pine 2 x 4 frames. there were not chunks of rubble nor gravel nor overgrown weeds found around the building. long, rusted steel girders did not protrude from the remnants of its roof. a faded sign above its entrance did not say, "wurlitzer juke boxes." muffled voices were not heard from within the structure. an argument about a drug deal did not become louder, and was not heard.

"where's da rest of da money?"

"i ain't gonna give it to ya! you screwed me on deals for the last time. i'm makin' up the difference this time."

"i think we can take care of that!"

"yeah, we ken take care of dis guy!"

"wait!...don't...oh my God!"

three shots were not heard from within the building. it did not sound as if a body thumped on the building's cement floor. more voices were not heard.

"let's get outta here."

"out the front so we won't look 'spicious."

"get the car out front."

"okay!"

41

"move it now!"

a large steel door did not creak open at the back of the building. a car did not start up. its engine did not rev hard. tires did not squeal from the back of the warehouse and gravel and dust were not spewed into the hot, dry air. a powder-blue and flat primer gray colored ford galaxy did not speed around the corner and screech to a stop in front at the entrance of the building. two large men in dark pinstriped suits with ties and hats did not come out of the front door. a faded paper sign posted did not say "no trespassing."

the driver of the car did not look around to see if there was anyone nearby. the two men did not settle in the back seat nor give the thumbs-up sign to each other as the car sped away. the tires did not screech down the highway, the wind did not not blow.

three police cars and an ambulance with a loud, shrill siren did not drive up to the building. it was not roped off by several officers with flat yellow warning cords. later, several men in blue suits and red ties did not walk in and out of the building. two ambulance drivers did not come out with a stretcher and a plastic bag that covered a lumpy mass which did not look about the width and length of a human being. officers did not inquire around the neighborhood regarding a recent drug related murder.

"did you see anything?"

"no," i didn't say. "nope, didn't not see a thing."

"yeah, that's not what i thought you'd didn't say," he never replied as he folded up his black note book and didn't not walk back towards the building.

just another story retold

"there was this man, you see,
a really great man..."

...said an old man who worked at the youth jail,
to this gang member, who had gotten out of a gang because he
said, "it was for real and they meant it when they hurt
people."

"so, like i was sayin', this really great man lived in a city,
and in that city there were these gangs,
and these gangs were more than part of that city,
the streets were theirs and they terrorized everyone,
seems some of the leaders of that city
moved them from the back alleys into the front streets,
and gave them gangs all kinds of rights,
rights to get whatever they could from the peoples,
and even gave them cool clothes to wear,
and other things like weapons and tatoos
which gave them even more power,
and the rest of the people hated it but had no choice,
until this man said, 'no!'

" 'no!'
to all the stuff that them gangs were doing to people,
as he tore up the places where the moneys were,
he threatened to take 'em all on,
if they didn't stop fucking around with people,
see, this guy was great,
and some of the people started to listen to him,
the gangs heard about this crazy guy who stood up to them,
and they priced his dead head,

43

after all it was their business,
and their streets,
to control and to terrorize
and no fool was gonna stop them,
because it would be bad for business if nobody was afraid to
die."

the boy swallowed hard.

"so the gangs found the man,
who went crazy on their turf,
and they told him to listen good, or else!
well, the man said, 'no,' to them,
so they gave him the, 'or else!'
and they killed him,
after hurting him real bad..."

...said the old man to the boy who was now listening this
time and thought about what the old man had said.

"do you know who i 'm talkin' about?
do you want to know who it was?
who it was they killed for sayin' no?
do you, huh?
well, you're like him some ways,
'cause you said, 'no!'
but you got out,
you got...out,
alive,
and lucky you,"

...said the old man as the boy smiled a little bit because
the old man cared about him long enough to tell him the story

and, well, nobody had talked to him in a while and it
was nice, and then the old man said...

"you know who be that man who said, 'no,'
and meant it?"

"no."

"oh for Christsakes, what's wrong with you, boy?"

the edge

downtown, an old neighborhood bar. close to the homes and back alleys of extra blue-collar workers. people stuck, methodical manner, the daily routine of "yet another day of the same old shit."

living, thriving on a bland diet of dull monotony and colorless skies, lost eyes, windows with drawn shades and burned-out neon lights of empty souls.

daily, each day they arise to fulfill existence burning time away in the factories of their minds, their lives, their everything. clouded in a veil of uncertainty and reluctant acceptance of each stillborn day.

inside, all seemed lost until that little corner bar opened up sometime back, though they all don't ever remember not ever having that little bar to stop in to socialize and forget. forget they do and the man who runs that place helps you to forget...your dreams that is. he'll still remind you of your hopeless situation.

that bar, like you. it is gray and light less, like the owner. yet, he always knows how you feel. he always knows a little more than you'd care for him to know in that small quaint establishment. the only lonely place where people can go to forget.

forgetting and all is forgotten. the passions of life, of dreams. lost hope and nobody cares about nothing anymore. yet, somehow this place is always packed full of people.

people, patrons who don't usually make sense, except in that sleepy enchantment of a forgotten nightmare.

suddenly, after the first draft, all the people who go there connect and start to make sense, as each person in turn reflects on their own dismal decay: this thing called life. how does it feel to feel your body dying after each minute?

46

one. one thought of each person stares at you from behind the mirrors. and one starts to wonder the purpose of it all and yet one cannot leave the bar stool or the booth. the bartender returns, you drink, and all is forgotten.

orders? "want another?" "yeah, give me another. what was my question? what was my purpose? i guess it doesn't matter does it?" a soft voice of doubt agrees, then the glass is refilled with some form of alcohol. tastes as peculiar as the addiction. the empty addiction of doing nothing about anything anyhow. sipping life away without incident. slowly.

again. it happens each time someone orders another draught of barley hops and mountain dew drops, or something a little harder, drinks concocted to take the edge off of living. and everything settles like the foam on the beer or the ice in the glass, or the backwash of the shot glass, or the dry heaving vomit of life.

and, all of life's journeys dead end here. here where apathy runs crisp and clean from a cute chrome mermaid's tit: the top to the keg's tap, pouring elixirs imported straight from hell.

*all, a*nd all makes sense. for hell has franchised itself and opened up a few little bars here and there. downtown. all set up to serve the selfish people of the darkened twilight. the shadows and shades of gloomy self dejection. welcome to hell! no, it's not down there, but here.

"*is* this what you ordered?" the soft voice crept up from behind the bar and served you again. yet you accept and suddenly feel uncertain whether you have or have not ordered. "whoever said we could control our feelings anyway? you can't order happiness? can you? where was i ? i forgot?"

lost. maybe you'll stay lost in your thoughts. yes, that's it. nevertheless. drink to it! toast it! for bub beezle or b.b. for short will serve you up whatever it is you think you need. a shot of sadness and a chase of pain. or maybe a tall cool glass of apathy–the kind of feeling that flows from your head to your feet and tingles your fingers, as it sends chills up and down your spine whenever you drink or think about how you've missed out because of others' better luck. destiny is cruel. blessings don't count especially in here. you can't even drink wine because of some old tradition. that and love. the only thing not served here. you can't order it in your own life, anyway. so why try ordering it here? it's not available anymore. obsolete. don't even ask. but still, here's the place to quench most empty consuming thirsts.

　　forever! as the bartender sets you up with another round.

　　cheers!

let's get lost

late, too late, i had had enough,
enough of the city, and i was alone,
living among the dead,
down the cliche, the lost street of broken dreams,
and past pasts,
and some old rusted abandoned cars
that didn't run no more,
down, way down the mean street,
of this generic concrete and iron town,

it is there i lived, and had nearly given up,
lost, in some childlike fairy tale of sadly never after,
near a church whose bells fell off,
but now played harsh notes through electric loudspeakers,
near a freeway off-ramp marked exit,
with flickering lights of faceless neighbors driving by,
near a die shop working the graveyard shift,
with brittle-crunching factory noises,
and down near the river,
which ran alongside of some oil refineries,
machines: modern sulfur burning dragons,
spewing and belching hellish flames,
high atop the toxic, waste-gas jet towers,
hymn of the american industrial night.

and through the deep cries of fallen angels,
now purposeless,
and cries of the babies not being fed,
and lonely cries of the drunks drinking time away,
and discorded songs of families fighting,
the rhythm of the night,

the slow sad song dripped heavy,
with the lost emotions of our numb generation,
immune to the past and to the now,
but not the unforgiving future,
the dirge somehow simply ended,
and i awoke to silence,
the piper had called me to join him,

my eyes were filled with dread,
in the city i lived,
lived and died a thousand jillion times,
but it was different this time,
uncharacteristic, unnatural, more human,
hard-edged and dark,
a silence i 'd never heard before,
mesmerized, frozen,
i thought for a moment that i could believe again,

but i didn't,
i couldn't find the questions,
and i couldn't bear the answers,
as i became one with the dark city's lost street,
unable to escape its' randomness, its' luck,
its' humanly murders,
the ecstatic faces of bitterness and pain,
the people who lived their lives, their lies,
the stereotypical, archetypal,
one dimensional fairy tale creatures,
the fuckin' court jesters, the fools,
the not-so-handsome princes,
and the sad princess whores,
hiding behind masks,
but hiding from what?

50

their emotions, their truths, their mortalities?
from the realities of the scary city at night,

let's get lost i thought,
and i was gone, driven,
my dirty muse saw me, played for me, played me,
through the pulses of the city streets, visions,
it's unnatural music,
the death march, the dirge
of the night traffic noises returned,
breaths, heartbeats,
everything and anything with rhythm,
i went,

i drove,
snaked my way through this un-eden,
down every highway, street,
avenue, road, and back alley and garden path,
past stop lights that didn't work,
past yellow flashing warning lights that did,
they blinked at me forever,
but this time i didn't listen to them, i had to ride,
nobody was around,
not a sad soul walked anywhere,
empty streets and my dark heart,
all went black,
the street-lights were all broken,
and there wasn't anything to look up to,
i was alone,
and now,

i never should have gone,
never should have gone and lived in the city,

in this never-ever land,
this place of broken concrete and fallen angels,

then my car overheated,
broken down,
and i kicked and kicked at my tires,
and the rush of the steam and pain and heat,
contrasted against the fog of the cool night air,
and everything changed and i saw it all,
the vision:
the city, it was perfect and i feared that the most,
there were no broken street pieces,
the road was good, new, golden,
each street glistened and shimmered and sparkled,
shiny new and it suddenly filled me with hope,
the city may work after all,
if the streets were fixed again, not just patched,
somehow,
and if the street lights worked, bright once more,
but how and who and when?

i got out of my car and walked,
block after block after block,
around and round,
i safely walked the unsafe city streets,
until i ended up,
where i had begun,

i knew the cities looked beautiful on the maps,
colorful, imaginative, but far away, lies,
true lies, i thought,
for i now know the city,
and i now know the answers,

in a breath i knew it all,
each piece fit perfectly when together,
and i got back to my car which suddenly ran,
and i rode the roads to the angels,
where all streets dead-end.

death by time

God rest ye dreary gentle world,
your time has come to pass,
the thirteenth hour has arrived,
as bells ring for lost mass,
the churches ring their somber notes,
as priceless moments end,
oh, tidings of mourning and grief,
mourning and grief,
oh tidings of lost beliefs,

long live the city, hurray!
long live the city, hurray!

the bricks, the very scales of the dragon shake,
and move and rattle and glow,
once and for all,
the fires of the legendary beast begin to flicker and sizzle,
as streets crumble and factories burn to the grounds,
the kracken then awakens to the end,
this time we will naught hear the laughter of the child,
as he appeared to before us with wisdom and warnings,
not this time,

to dust, sandy dust,
we return,
for we, sons of adam went forth and named everything,
and the wrecking ball of time will come,
to tear down the last wall,
and all we will watch and all we will mourn,

the four horsemen will not be stopped at the borders this time,

then the acid rains will come and melt away the city,
as we,
the last generation of users,
used up everything,
saving nothing, even our grace,

whilst the kings and queens with all their silver and gold,
couldn't put humpty together again,
as black witches cast spells to try and stop the asphalt plagues
that surrounded the concrete forests,
and the reclamation of the city began,
and the weeds grow between the cracks and crevices,
breaking apart the very foundation of our sad experiment.

street dreams

it's pumpkin time!
in the meanest of mean cities,
and all good little girls and boys
should be home by now,
from balls, banquets,
gala grown-up, dress up affairs,
or whatever the hell you do these days,
but never mind,
croaks the raven
never mind.

it's late, so bed-dy bye
sweet prince, fair princess, good night,
sleep tight, safely tucked away in bed,
now and forevermore,
safe from the nighttime traffic noises,
street ogres, rogues, wags, and wolves,
and the robin goodfellows,
all living, dying, breathing in the 'hood,
those special people who might make sport of you,
and steal your precious, pre-planned futures,
your dreams and slit your throats leaving you quite dead,
croaked the raven,
forevermore.

yet the traffic throbs outside
on the meanest of streets,
it hurts your numb ears,
the haunting screams rend from the blackest
unraven-like darkness
of the city at night,

56

heedless, sleep sweetly,
safe, in your immune contentious consciousness,
the street lamps glare their pathetic unglares,
their unlights,
through your polluted window panes,
intensify the pain of your day,
the aches, the bustle of exhausted and exerted anxieties
come at night to play havoc on your restless mind,
and you with your kerchiefs or caps,
settle down for a long hell's winter nap,

shadows move, seethe as you breathe, dream, writhe,
heave with the stress of your day,
as you grope, hope to understand your unknown purposes,
the reasons for your existence,
of your average eighty-five year life sentence,
until the angel overtakes you,
and finally brings your peace,

but do try to sleep, if you can?
can you? cannot? damn it!
deal with the problems of the city,
your life, the unlife of the flat world as it spins,
counterclockwise, against the tides and winds,
as the city goes on, forever forward and backward,
but still onward,
evolve, devolve,
in our uncity,
the revolution of hope was lost,
our ancestors would have been proud,
modern unman, modern unwoman,

we, last lost generation of cave dwellers,

huddled in bank-owned cement, brick, aluminum
shelters, helter skelter,
surrounded by the city, trapped, locked in,
and we make proud use of our short time,
worship our one dimensional demigods,
soothe the salvation of our emptiness,
the visions of our unlife,
as the shadows bleed from day to night,

the social drama unfolds,
and yet you cannot sleep?
why not watch a little t.v.?
the information age blitzes us
a million channels of zip,
turn it on, tune out,
why not eat microwave dinners, you know,
the ones that taste just like grandma used to zap?
then watch whatever we want,
remotely, change feelings we don't want to show,
stop it! change it!
can't, it's life, and we can't,
sparked the electrical raven,
until now and forevermore,

and all of this brought to you by those happy fucks
who sell you pizza,
during special reports on starvation,
who promote money as the answer to everything,
and the lottery as its' means,
yes! play for a future,
bring up a family in style,
in the comfort unzone of worry free freedom,
the ridiculous sale price of reality,

fuck the commercials!
we don't really want to watch starvation anyway,
get a video instead, make it cool,
something you've only seen
a hundred times before,
it's the unlife of the uncity,
forevermore,
and it's unfair, the unfair,
so change it or turn it off,
yes! off! off to bed now,
are we in wet dreamland yet?
did we say our gimme gimme materialistic prayers yet?
no more glasses of water,
no pills to sleep,
go to bed! get to sleep!
good night damnit!
good night again!
whispered the raven but i want more,
forevermore,

how about maybe a 'bed-dy bye' story,
to ease us into sleep,
another street piece to tell,
a children's bedtime story,
my dear lost sweet soul,
relax for a safe street dream,
croaked the raven,
tell me more, tell me more.

the dustman cometh, who you say?
the dream-master, again, who? you say,
the sandman, not the reaper, but his friend,
the one from the uncity,

who'll actually come into the 'hood at night,
where darkness is enlightening,
who? you ask thrice,
as the raven crowed three times,
it is he,
the only one who ever comes into this 'hood,
maybe he'll bring his bag of pills,
nice magic pills to make you sleep,
dream if you dare,
as he creeps softly,
the whispering wind behind your door,
under your bed,
inside your head! hide your head!
snarled the raven,
forevermore,
until death and forevermore.

lay down, listen...that's him,
keep your eyes closed or he won't come,
shh! he did it,
you're almost here or there now,

sweet dreams, oh yes, so sweet,
but heed his advice,
don't dream of streets,
street dreams, mean dreams,
wicked victories of the howling night,

how about a long lost story
of a great nighttime journey,
into the abandoned parts of the city,
too late, you're dreaming about the nighttime city,
and you cannot awake,

60

you are carried off to the distant unsun,
the industrial waste of nevermore,
as we go on in life,
the unlife of the unfair city,
circle the square blocks,
faster, faster, end up nowhere, still faster,
shrieked the raven,
nowhere, but here,

here in the city,
night without pity,
you may not awake from this dream,
you may not awake in the morn,
if you sleep here,
in the city,
but there's always hope,
it depends on what you hope for,
the reaper hopes you'll die,
the sandman hopes you'll dream,
and all must realize,
you were born to die
the moment after your birth,
short time, lifetimes are short,
to find whatever is our purpose?
sighed the raven,
whatever for?

the street gangs paint graffiti night pieces,
as you ride the nightmares of the unnight,
and the unsweetened dreams of life,
here in the loneliest place called now,
be with the people of the edge,
when shallow daylight,

melts into the shadows of the night,
and not in your hands,
but in your mouth,
as you swallow what's left of light,
dangle your feet over the edge,
ah, skip a few stones into the abyss,
and listen to the flapping wings,
as the raven caws,
how lost,
for now and forevermore.

for the city,
the lost mean city
stirs, awakens,
as we try once again to sleep,
perchance, to dream,
sweet dreams, street dreams,
safe in your bed and in your dreams,
or so you thought...

hello! hurray!
let the lights grow dim!
let the show begin!
are you ready?
ladies, gentlemen, children of all ages,
welcome!
step right up, don't be afraid now,
you, hey you, come now, give us a try,
try living in the city of your daydreams,
as reality rides into this fair city,
to it's annual city fair,

hurry! hurry! hurry!

see the show of shows,
the daily carnivorous carnal carnival,
the sideshow:
freak show of unpeople, unfreaks,
undreams of the unnight,
dark as dark,
as dark as the undarkest dark alleys ever unlit before,
where the street lamps never go off,
lending sight of an unnatural light,
to the unlight of the uncity,

twinkle, twinkle,
little fucking neon star,
how we wonder,
what the fuck is what?
up above the 'hood those useless lights so high,
how we wonder,
you survive,

to pay this price thrice, again, then again,
lose at the games of life,
and think how really fuckin' unfair
the city truly is,
the ungreen, the colorful unlights of the city,
freaks of the enrapture,
committing the unspeakable,
all for only a nickel,
all for your pleasure,
if then pleasure you seek, pleasure you shall reap,
so double your pleasure,
double your fun,
for one thin dime,
sorry the price just went up,

how unfair you thought,
after all this is the unfair of the uncity,
and after all,
who cares?
quoth the raven,
who cares?

but look, quick, peek,
see the woman with her long hair in curlers:
rapunzel escaping the trapped castle life
by going out with her baby,
very very late at night,
maybe she needed milk
for her child who cries?
medicine? something very important
for the sake of the child we're sure
but shouldn't she ought to wait?
until it's daylight and safe?
yet here she comes this mother and her child,
walking down the sidewalk,
towards the neon lights of the late night carryout,
with some mean looking drunks,
princes of the darkness standing around,
and sayin' nothing, hanging out,
who knows?
keep walking friend,
from the abyss, don't stray,
but who cares about her anyways?
with dirty pink slippers,
not made of glass, i bet,
her hair in a rag,
she stumbles up the broken stoop,
inside she goes, while outside her child knows,

64

is to stay,
afraid, alone, cold, tired,
but mom comes out, with her paper bag,
a glass bottle which explains everything away,
and she lights a fresh pack and heads back,
to whatever tale she runs from,

remember my pretties,
it is only a dream,
as we cross the rivers of our minds,
where the styx, the stoners,
sling rocks of sugar crack candy,
and would break your bones and leave you rotting,
for the ambulance ravens to carry your carrion body,
to the coroner on call,
and the butcher's autopsy
of your end,
as if anyone would be bothered
on this carnival of night,

sweet morning comes and somehow you luck out,
it was only a bad dream,
there, there, feel better?
you're awake, you're alive,
but sick from the toxic levels of the darkness,
so much more wiser,
in the meanest of mean cities,
amazing!
but life is both good and bad,
and the city dreams of people who survive
in the wonderful loony humanness
of the silent night of the city.
and the raven croaks,

nevermore,
and hopes for your tomorrow.
sang the raven,
depressus extollor, depressus extollor...

kites

the wind blew,
across the back alleys,
and sweeping hills,
and broken glass,
and garbage,
of the razed property,
on a small lot,
in the inner-inners of a city,

the angels were in the clouds
on that particularly odd spring day,
and for a moment,
the stench, and the death,
and the emptiness of the city full of people,
left, and the sirens blew not,
only the winds,

only the winds,
the winds of the warm early spring,
and we sat out on the back fire escape,
and we talked,
and remembered dreaming,
and tried to hum songs of hope,
but we forgot the tunes
as we watched three kids,
on that old back lot,
trying to fly a kite,
they probably stole,

but it was great, great, lost fun,
that we had somehow forgot,

and we were sad because we forgot,
as the wind blew,
out on the back fire escape,
across the open lot,

God! we thought, let's fly back,
back to the naive and white clouds and lost angels
of our youth.